W0007790

First published by the Ministry of Information in 1943

First published in 2007 in this format by
IWM, Lambeth Road, London SE1 6HZ
This edition printed 2015

iwm.org.uk

ISBN 978-1-904897-65-1

Printed and bound in China by Imago Publishing

Contents

Issued for the Ministry of Health
and the Central Council for Health Education
by the Ministry of Information

First Published, 1943
Crown Copyright Reserved

Price 3d. net, or 10s.0d. for 50 copies

Foreword

by the Minister of Health

~~~~~~

DURING three years of total war the nation's stubborn good health has been invaluable to our war effort. Even so, as a nation we are still losing about 22 million weeks' work each year through common and often preventable illnesses such as colds and influenza, dyspepsia, biliousness, neurasthenia, rheumatism, boils and other septic conditions. This is calculated to be equivalent to the loss of 24,000 tanks, 6,750 bombers, and 6,750,000 rifles a year, not to mention the pain and inconvenience we suffer as individuals. We cannot expect, whatever we do, to wipe out this loss completely, but we can all do something to reduce it. And now that we are at the turning point of the war it is more than ever important that we should do everything we can to keep fit—fit to hasten victory and to tackle the tasks that lie beyond. But to maintain vigorous health calls for conscious effort from each one of us. In this little book Dr. Clegg has set out the simple safeguards, the common sense rules, and the good habits which we can make part and parcel of our daily lives. By doing so we shall both help ourselves to health and help to keep the nation fighting fit.

Ernest Brown

HOW TO KEEP WELL IN WARTIME

by H. A. CLEGG, MB., M.R.C.P.

1. Be Regular in Your Living Habits

A watchmaker will tell you that a watch will keep better time if it is wound up at the same hour each day. The sun rises and sets at regular intervals. With unfailing regularity spring comes after winter. Nature sets us an example in being regular in her habits. If we rebel and become irregular in our habits, we pay for it in the long run.

Don't think that to be healthy you have to be one of the "big muscle boys." A world made up of heavy-weight champions would be a dull place. What you want to aim at is a smooth working of body and mind. A jerky fitfulness of behaviour, of activity, will disturb yourself and those near you.

That is why the first rule of health is to be regular in the habits of living —eating, sleeping, resting, working, emptying the bowels. On a basis of regular habits that self-discipline without which no man can take his full share as a citizen in a civilized community comes easier. Of course, too much regularity can become rather dull, but there is plenty of room for an occasional breakaway. A last-minute decision to go on an excursion, to have a picnic, to visit a friend, often increases the pleasure of the event. Slavish following of a routine is just as harmful as continually living on the impulse of the moment.

"That sounds very nice," you may say, especially if you are a wife and mother—"but there is a war on. We had an air raid last night. The children have to be got off early, so that I can go to the factory. And my husband goes to work earlier still. We live rather a long way from it."

The woman in the home has a thousand and one difficulties to face. Her man, too, has his family anxieties, and he wants to put all he has into his work. Her health, his health, the health of their children are important to the nation to which they belong, and to themselves as individuals. So the extra effort that may be needed to keep the family's habits as regular as possible in face of such difficulties is well worth while.

Start the Day Well. Try to have your meals at the same time each day. This is particularly important for children. At all events, make a good start by having breakfast punctually, and early enough to give everyone in the house a chance to go to the w.c. before work or school. Half the stomach troubles people have begin because they don't give their bowels a chance to open properly after breakfast. A hurried breakfast, bolted rather than eaten, not enough time for a visit to the w.c., a rush for tram, train, or bus—what a thoroughly bad start for the day's work!

If you are troubled with constipation, correct it by attention to diet, habit, and exercise. Do not take drugs for it unless your doctor thinks they are necessary. Eat more vegetables. Drink a glass of water first thing in the morning, and give yourself time.

2. Get Enough Sleep

It is possible that you begin the day badly by ending yesterday badly—that is by going to bed too late. It is true that some people can do with less sleep than others. But the average adult should try to have eight hours' sleep every night, so if you get up at 6 a.m., try to be in bed with the lights off by 10 p.m. A weekly night on fire guard or A.R.P. won't do you any harm if you make up the lost sleep during the week.

People who find it hard to go to sleep are often those who find it hard to relax. They are too tense, too restless, too "nervy". Or it may be that if you find it difficult to fall off to sleep you have "something on your mind"—a domestic worry, anxiety about money, about health. Try to find out what this something is, and then take steps to settle the matter that is worrying you. In any case, try *not* to worry about things you *cannot* change. Here are some tips that may help those who suffer from sleeplessness.

This May Help You to Sleep. If you have been working indoors all day, a quarter of an hour's walk in the open air before bedtime may give you a pleasant feeling of mental relaxation that will quickly bring on sleep. Some people are helped by a hot bath, others by a hot drink (but not tea or coffee), just before going to bed. Others, again, send themselves to sleep by reading a book—a rather stodgy book, not a detective tale.

You won't go to sleep easily if you are too hot or too cold. And you won't sleep healthily if the windows are closed. So open the windows wide, in all weathers except fog, just before getting into bed, and keep warm by putting over yourself more blankets, or a dressing gown, or an overcoat. People who suffer from cold feet should put on socks. A hot water bottle, remember, means extra consumption of fuel, unless you can put your kettle on a fire already in use for heating or cooking. Noise is another disturber of sleep, as you'll know if you're on night shift. Ear plugs, or cotton-wool and vaseline, will help to keep noise out.

Someone in your household may suffer badly from insomnia, and feel run down as a result. In this case seek a doctor's advice. And don't lose sleep worrying about what the doctor will think of you if you go to him. Of course he's busier than usual in wartime and he appreciates considerate treatment, but the National Health Insurance Scheme was invented to make it easier for you to have the benefit of his advice when you really need it.

How Much Sleep Your Children Need. Children need more sleep than adults because they use up so much energy in growing. In summer-time, with its extra hours of daylight, parents find it difficult to get their children to bed. But remember this table:

Age in years				Hours of sleep needed
1	...	...	...	14–16
2–3	...	...	...	12–14
4–5	...	...	...	10–12
6–10	...	...	...	10–11
11–16	...	...	...	$9\frac{1}{2}$–10

Few things are more important to a child than the right amount of rest and sleep, and modern parents are apt to let their children stay up too late. So you must be firm in this matter. See that the curtains in the room in which your children sleep are well drawn, so that the daylight does not get in. Arrange the beds so that the children sleep with their heads turned away from the window. Once they are asleep and it is dark, you can draw back the curtains so that more air can come into the room.

3. Get Your Share of Air and Sunshine

The black-out makes it less easy to keep rooms well ventilated. But there are one or two obvious points not always borne in mind. The first is that, provided there is not a strong wind, it is not always necessary to shut the windows when you draw the curtains at black-out time. This depends to some extent on how the curtains are placed. You can see whether air currents disturb the black-out by going outside and looking. If your curtains only just fill the space of the window frame, then you might use one of the many devices that give you good ventilation *and* proper black-out. They are based on the fact that air can get round corners but light cannot. If you live in a bed-sitting room, air the room until it is smoke-free before you get into bed.

Why Ventilation is Important. You should pay the greatest attention to ventilation. There is no doubt that we feel better and are better if the rooms in which we work, eat, and sleep are well ventilated. Headaches, lassitude, lack of appetite may all result from a stuffy room, especially from the dead atmosphere of a centrally heated one. It does not matter so much that the air should be fresh as that it should be on the move.

Remember that you yourself are a furnace, continually stoked by food. In the combustion of food in your body—for example, by your muscles when you do physical work—heat is given off. You are a warm-blooded animal and your body is kept at a temperature above that of the air round you. Your normal temperature, as you may know, is 98·4° F., when taken under the tongue. (The temperature of your liver is in the region of 100° F.) An average comfortable indoor temperature, whether in shop, office, or living-room, is about 60° to 65° F. So, being hotter than the air round you, you will always be losing heat to it, just as hot water added to cold water will become less hot by losing heat to it. The cold water, of course, becomes warmer.

Still Air Means Stuffy Rooms. If you could not lose the heat produced in your body you would die of heat-stroke; you would simply boil over. The chief way in which you lose heat is by the evaporation of water from your skin and lungs. When you get very hot you lose such a lot of water that it forms into visible drops on your skin—as sweat. If the air is very moist then it will not be able to take up much moisture from your body. And if it is still as well it will not be able to carry away the heat you are giving out. With still, moist air round you, your temperature will tend to rise and you will feel hot, stuffy, and uncomfortable. So keep the air on the move. If the working process of mill or foundry demands a higher temperature than 65° you will need more than ever to get all the fresh air you can when not at work.

In your living-rooms at home keep the air on the move and the temperature at a moderate level; over-heated rooms are inadvisable from the point of view of both health and fuel economy.

Sun-and-air Baths. If you are lucky you may spend your brief annual holiday in a burst of sunshine.

But holiday or no, seize every opportunity you can of giving your skin a good airing. The air "bath" is just as important as the sun "bath". The sun bath can be taken in your garden just as well as at the seaside. This is worth remembering now that most of us have to take our holidays at home. The play of sun and air on the bare skin is stimulating and generally tones you up, especially if you have a sluggish circulation. The ultraviolet rays of the sun act on a fatty substance in your skin and turn it into Vitamin D, the anti-rickets vitamin. This makes it possible for children to have strong and well-formed bones. If it is very hot and you sit in the shade, the ultra-violet rays will still reach your skin from the clear blue sky.

Precautions for Sun-bathers. You can have too much of a good thing, and you can have too much sun; you can in fact get sun-stroke, and your temperature will rise, as in a fever. Or you may just get sun-burn, and blisters will come up on your red and inflamed skin.

So, next summer, start sun-bathing gradually. And don't do it in the heat of the day, but in the early part of the morning and the latter part of the afternoon. Don't sit in the sun immediately after a meal. Young children and old people should take especial care, and blondes should remember that as a rule they can stand the sun less well than brunettes. Those with weak hearts and weak chests, too, must be careful, because undue exposure to the sun may make their troubles worse. Young children and old people should have a covering over the head and the back of the neck. The sun-bather should begin by exposing himself—first one side then the other—for, say, ten minutes on the first occasion. Then, as he or she begins to brown, the exposure can be increased. But to grill oneself can do nothing but harm.

4. Keep Mind and Body Active

Those who can get to the seaside in wartime are lucky. There, in addition to sun and air, they can expose their bodies to sea-water. There are few better ways of exercising the body than swimming, whether in the sea, the river, or in the local baths. Here again the temptation is to overdo it. It is stupid to stay in the water until your fingers and toes go white or blue. There is really no point in showing off to your friends and relations by swimming just too far just a bit too often.

Whether you take your exercise, by walking, by

cycling, by swimming, by gardening, or by playing games, there is always one sign that will tell you when you are overdoing it—that is, undue fatigue amounting to exhaustion. This is quite different from a healthy tiredness after exercise, which gives you at the same time a feeling of relaxation. A sense of exhaustion means that you have done yourself harm instead of good.

Holidays at Home. For your spare time and your holiday you should aim at two things. The first is relaxation. The second is change. Change itself will help you to relax. And it need not be a drastic change. For years you may not have visited that place only three or four miles from where you live. You may not have been to a concert or a theatre for months or even years. Possibly you have never thought of looking in at the public library.

Don't spend all your time over billiards or cards in a heavy, smoky atmosphere. Do something different. There are many things you can do that will bring change and refreshment into your life, even if the war makes it advisable for you to spend your holiday at home.

Make the Most of Spare Time. It is just as

necessary to relax, mentally and physically, during the ordinary working week. The best way of doing this will vary according to circumstances. If your work is of the hard manual kind your muscles will be tired and what you need most perhaps is actual rest. If your job keeps you standing all day or if it involves monotonous repetition, you probably need a change, such as walking, more than rest. (Girls and women should wear low heels for standing and walking.) If you sit all day in an office or a workshop you won't be physically or muscularly tired but you may feel jaded and too tired to take exercise.

What is needed, whatever your work, is change of activity, something that will exercise those of your muscles that you haven't been using during the day, and won't be using on your Home Guard parade or in your Civil Defence duties.

For most of us exercise is essential if health is to have a polish on it. If possible some form of exercise should be taken daily in the open air. One way of doing this is to get up half an hour earlier in the morning, and walk part of the way to work. If you are not too tired at the end of the day you might also walk part of the way back. During this war many people have begun to cycle to work and have felt better for it.

Muscles are Meant to be Used. Those masses of muscle on arm, leg, thigh, back, and belly are not just ornamental. They are there to be used. If they are not used they will sooner or later let you know about it. Muscular rheumatism is a common complaint in this country, and one precaution to take against it is to keep joints and muscles on the go so that the blood flows freely through them. Are your muscles becoming set? Can you, standing with knees straight, touch the tips of your toes with the tips of your fingers? Try it. In your weekends, when you can, walk, cycle, swim, dig, row a boat, and enjoy it. Don't put it off. Start now, and never mind feeling stiff to begin with.

Advice to the Fat. If you are overweight you must start your exercise gradually, and increase it gradually. It is true that some people are fat by nature. In others fatness may be the result of disease. In many people fatness is the result of a combination of over-eating and lack of exercise. A man called Daniel Lambert created what must be a record of fatness. He weighed 52 stone and his waist measurement was 9 feet 4 inches. He died before he was forty. Insurance companies say that fat men do not live so long as thin men.

If you are overweight and feel that your health is not up to scratch, seek your doctor's advice before you do anything about it. Whatever you do, do *not* take slimming tablets or thyroid tablets without a doctor's prescription. People have died from taking tablets supposed to make them slim.

The usual advice to the fat who want to get thin is to tell them to eat less, especially of sweet and starchy foods. In these days of rationing any adjustment of your diet had better be carried out carefully. You need not, of course, eat your ration of sweets. But concentrate on taking more exercise, and begin gradually.

Advice to those Underweight. Being too thin is little better than being too fat. In young women, in particular, leanness is no advantage. Unfortunately, during recent years it has become fashionable for girls and young women to be slim, and they usually manage this by eating too little, rations or no rations. Young women, especially, should eat their full ration, because tuberculosis is commoner among them than among other people. Under-feeding, especially of fats, gives tuberculosis a chance to obtain a hold on a person. There are, by the way, no such things as "slimming foods".

5. Choose the Right Food

It is probable that you already know a lot about food and food values. One of the benefits of this war is the more intelligent interest everyone has taken in food, thanks to necessity and the efforts of the Ministry of Food. If your interest has been aroused, please keep it up now, and when peace comes. Much misery has been caused by faulty feeding and by ignorance of food facts. Thousands upon thousands have died because of such ignorance.

For example, in the East, natives living largely on polished rice die of a disease called beri-beri. This is because the vitamin which protects against this disease—vitamin B1—is thrown away with the husks polished off the rice. In the Philippines some 18,000 people died of beri-beri in 1925.

Scientists and doctors are not just being faddy, therefore, when they are anxious that everyone should every day eat enough of the protective foods—the foods that protect against diseases like beri-beri, rickets, and scurvy. Let it be said at once that if you take a good mixed diet—and you can still do so in spite of food rationing—you need not worry about whether you are having enough of this or that. But you must know what is "good".

The Source of all Your Energy. It is becoming rather hackneyed to compare the human body to a machine. But the comparison is a useful one, because most of what is known about the way the body works can be explained on mechanical principles. The engineer can work out that in certain conditions a car will give a certain performance when petrol vapour undergoes combustion in the engine's cylinders. Part of the energy freed by the combustion moves the piston and the car "goes". Part of the energy is given off as heat and this warms up the water in the radiator.

The fuel for *your* engine is food. Combustion takes place inside the body. Part of the energy freed is used by your muscles and you "go". Part is given off as heat and warms your blood. The amount of energy that various foods will give can be exactly calculated. The amount of energy and heat you produce in your body can be measured. And it is easily proved that this energy and this heat come from the combustion of food and nothing else. You cannot, so to speak, create energy.

Oxygen Feeds You, Too. Just as petrol vapour must be mixed with air for it to make the car go, so do you need air. For combustion to take place, oxygen is necessary. You obtain this from the air you breathe.

The oxygen in the air which goes to the lungs passes into the blood. The blood carries the oxygen to every part of the body. Without oxygen—without combustion—the body cannot do its work, and so it dies.

How the Body Burns up Sugar. If sugar is burnt outside the body it finally turns into water and carbon dioxide—the gas that gives the fizz to soda water. Exactly the same thing happens in the body. The carbon dioxide is carried by the blood to the lungs, and you breathe it out into the air. (Incidentally, plants use the carbon dioxide in the air as food for themselves.) Some of the water, too, is breathed out of the lungs. But water also leaves the body through the skin as sweat and by the bladder and bowels as urine and faeces.

Combustion of sugar gives the body a quick supply of energy. When you do brain work—read, speak, or listen, for example—the cells in your brain burn up sugar, and for this they need oxygen. The oxygen is carried by the red corpuscles in your blood. If you have too few red corpuscles —if you are anaemic— then your brain may not get enough oxygen and therefore won't work so well.

So, in a sense, oxygen is a food, and that is one reason why doctors want people to have plenty of fresh air in well-ventilated houses, offices and factories. In some illnesses doctors give the patient an extra amount of oxygen to breathe.

Everyone Needs Starch. Sugar and starch are what chemists call carbohydrates. Starch is an important food. It is the chief stuff in bread, potatoes, and all cereal foods. During digestion it is broken down into sugar, which is a simpler chemical substance. So whether you eat starch or sugar it is all the same in the long run because they both enter the blood from the intestines as the sugar called glucose. But when you eat starch, for example, in the form of the National loaf, you obtain other useful things as well, such as Vitamin B and iron. And in potatoes you get Vitamin C.

Foods to Round Off the Corners. You probably know that the other two foodstuffs used by the body for energy and heat are fat and protein. Fat may be in the form of butter, margarine, milk, suet, dripping, herrings or salmon (fresh or tinned). Besides giving energy, fat also rounds off the corners of the body and sometimes makes them look attractive. It serves, too, as a food store and as an insulator against loss of heat. Protein—the lean of meat and the white of egg are protein (mixed of course with water)—is perhaps the most important of the three. Protein is the body builder. It is the principal ingredient in the billions of tiny cells which make up your body.

It may be said briefly that we eat starches, sugars, and fats for energy, and proteins so that we can build up the body and keep it in a good state of repair. Food experts say that animal protein is better for this purpose than vegetable protein (peas, beans, and oatmeal), and so call it "first-class". You get first-class protein from meat, fish, eggs, liver, milk, and cheese, *and in one of these forms you should have some first-class protein every day.*

War has reduced our supplies of first-class protein, so plan to make the most of your rations. If you have meat or fish for dinner, don't have cheese as well. Cheese, in wartime anyhow, should not be treated as a savoury tit-bit. It is a good solid food consisting largely of fat and protein, and first-class protein at that. Drink your full ration of liquid milk, and use dried milk in your puddings. And while dried eggs are obtainable use them for cooking, and keep your shell eggs for egg dishes. Keep an eye and an ear open for the Ministry of Food's hints in newspaper advertisements and broadcasts; they're scientifically planned to help to keep you fit.

Food for Blood and Bones. But fuel isn't everything in diet. You must have certain chemical elements like iron and calcium (or lime). Iron is necessary to make blood. If you don't eat enough iron you become anaemic. It is the iron that carries the oxygen in the blood. You obtain iron in various ways. It is present in the National loaf, in green leafy vegetables (especially spinach and watercress), in the yolk of egg, in liver and lean meat, and in peas and beans. If you become very anaemic the doctor may have to give you an iron medicine.

Calcium (lime) is important because it is the stuff from which bones and teeth are made. Your bones are alive. They, as well as other parts of the body, need calcium. Your muscles won't work efficiently without calcium. Without calcium the blood won't clot properly. Cheese and milk are good natural suppliers of calcium. When there is a shortage of milk, there is a risk that people will not obtain enough of this bone-builder in their diet. This may help you to understand why Lord Woolton has taken the doctors' advice to increase the cheese ration and add calcium to flour.

Vitamins Protect You. Just as calcium and iron are present in sufficient amount in a well-mixed ample diet, so are the vitamins. It is a pity vitamins are labelled with the letters of the alphabet. It makes them seem unreal and mysterious. But they are real enough, being rather complicated chemical substances made up of carbon, hydrogen, oxygen, nitrogen, and sulphur, especially of the first three of these. The chemist can now manufacture some of them in his laboratory—Vitamin C for example.

We need very small amounts of the vitamins, and only very small amounts of them exist in foodstuffs. But without vitamins the fuel—sugars and fats—in your body will be wasted. They will burn badly and there will be a lot of smoke. Vitamin A, for example, protects the eyes. Vitamin B keeps the skin clear and the nerves steady. Vitamin C saves you from scurvy, and Vitamin D from rickets. Vitamin E helps you to be fertile, and Vitamin K stops you from bleeding when you shouldn't. No wonder doctors call foods rich in vitamins "protective" foods.

Now all these and other vitamins are present in natural foods and always have been. Unfortunately, it has not always been possible for people to eat the right kind of foods, or they have been ignorant of what to eat. What you fancy does not necessarily do you good.

How to Get Your Vitamins. Eat as much as you can of the protective foods. You buy these at the greengrocer's, the dairy, and the fish shop. Milk, butter, cheese and eggs are available in varying and restricted amounts. So be sure each member of the family has his or her full ration of them, and see that the children get the extra ration of milk the Government provides to meet their special needs. The same applies to the expectant mother. The manufacturers add the "sunshine vitamins" A and D to margarine, so this can he classed as a dairy food. Cheese is a useful food for children, and cooking doesn't take away its goodness.

Vitamin D is not found in many foods, though there is some in fat fish (like herring and salmon), so unless fish-liver oils are taken we have to depend for Vitamin D largely on the action of sunlight on the skin. Therefore full advantage should be taken of the cod-liver oil obtainable from the Welfare Centres for expectant mothers and children under five. Eat fish when you can, especially fat fish, and especially herrings.

How to Replace the Vitamin in Oranges. Now that foreign fruits like oranges are, to say the least of it, scarce, you must make the most of what there is at home. Oranges and lemons were valuable chiefly because of the Vitamin C in them. There is a lot of Vitamin C in the good old-fashioned "two veg.", potatoes and cabbage; and in tomatoes, water-cress, parsley, broccoli, and swede turnip. If enough of these vegetables are eaten there need be no fear of scurvy, so long as the vegetables are properly prepared and cooked. For children under five Vitamin C in the form of concentrated orange juice is obtainable from Welfare Centres and from local Food Offices.

How to Cook Your Vegetables. You can waste your Vitamin C if you don't cook your vegetables properly. Here are some hints on cooking vegetables. Obtain them as fresh as possible. Keep them in a cool place and avoid crushing or bruising them. Prepare them only just in time for the meal. If you soak them before boiling them, add salt (2 teaspoonsful to a pint) to the water. When boiling vegetables use only just enough water to cover them. Bring the water to the boil and add salt before you put the vegetables in. Put them in gradually to prevent the water going off the boil: *don't* add baking soda (sodium bicarbonate).

Boil the vegetables just long enough to make them tender, not a moment longer. Serve them at once. Don't keep them warming up on the hot plate, because the longer vegetables are heated the more Vitamin C is destroyed. Lastly, use the water in which the vegetables have been boiled for soups or gravy.

Potatoes should be boiled or steamed in their skins.

Now that we are all digging for victory there should be plenty of vegetables. Don't cook them all, eat some raw every day as far round the year as possible. And remember that lettuce isn't the only salad vegetable. Mustard and cress, watercress, shredded cabbage, grated carrot, tomatoes, endive, young dandelion leaves, radish, parsley, and chives, are some of the vegetables that can go into the salad dish. From vegetables, cooked and raw, you get calcium, iron, and various salts and vitamins.

Wholesome Bread. Provided you take the largest amount possible of protective foods, you needn't worry much about what else you eat. In peacetime people tended to eat far too much sugar and refined cereals (including white bread). Wartime necessities should become peacetime habits. So when peace returns still go steady with the sugar, and still go on eating wheatmeal or brown bread. Russians eat black bread, and they're a tough lot. Wheatmeal bread, by the way, has safely been given to patients with stomach ulcers without upsetting their digestions.

Don't forget that food is meant to be enjoyed. The more you like it (without making a pig of yourself) the more good it will do you. You can't enjoy it to the full if it's badly cooked or badly served. Cooking is an art, and to cook well is something to be proud of.

Drink Enough Water. About 75 per cent, of your body is water. And if anyone talks to you about "dry bones" you can inform him that 25 per cent of the weight of a bone is contributed by water. When sugar is burnt in the body, to yield energy and heat, it is finally broken down to carbon dioxide and water. Three-quarters of the brain is water.

As has already been said, water is being lost at varying rates through the skin and the lungs, in the urine, and in the faeces. Water plays a vital part in all the chemical and physical changes in the body. Yet some people think it is just stuff to wash in.

Water is meant to be drunk. In fact you must drink it, or you would die of thirst. You should take some three pints a day. Most people like their water coloured rather than plain, even if the colour is only that of weak tea or bad coffee. Some people still like a glass of beer, though they will tell you that nowadays it is little better than coloured water. You can drink too much tea, too much coffee, too much beer. It can't be said that any of them do you any good. Too much always does harm. Few people drink enough water. So see that you get enough of it yourself.

6. Be Moderate in All Things

Drinks like tea, coffee, beer, gin, whisky, rum have their attractions, of course. A cup of tea often "bucks you up". But alcohol may act as a poison; it certainly does when an overdose is taken. A drunk person is a person poisoned with alcohol. The alcohol called "hooch" is such a strong poison that it blinds and even kills people. To take a glass of beer with a friend is a pleasant social custom. But don't delude yourself that beer does you good, because it doesn't.

Are We Smoking too Much? Another over-worked social custom is smoking. The consumption of tobacco went up by leaps and bounds at the beginning of the war. Tobacco may soothe the nerves, but it may also spoil the appetite and irritate the mouth, throat, and lungs. It can upset the digestion, and interfere with mental and physical efficiency. Two years before the war, in 1937, this country spent £150,000,000 on tobacco. There appear to be social virtues in smoking. It has certainly become a social habit, and in many cases a bad habit. Most people can quote examples of hale and hearty old men of 80 who have smoked all their lives without harm. And there is Mr. Churchill with his cigars. But these are exceptional men.

For the ordinary man and woman good health will not be theirs unless they smoke in strict moderation. King James I said of smoking that it is "a custom loathsome to the eye, hateful to the nose, harmful to the brain, dangerous to the lungs, and in the black stinking fume thereof nearest resembling the horrible stygian smoke of the bottomless pit". This was, of course, laying it on a bit thick.

Not a Cure for Nerves. There is no doubt that smoking too much and drinking too much are often due to "nervousness". The act of smoking seems to relieve a sense of strain—and in wartime everyone is living under some sort of strain. But, in excess, smoking makes the nervousness worse, apart from its harm to physical health. The effect of alcohol on the brain is to relieve stress and anxiety. As everyone knows, it makes a person less critical—of himself at all events. But the slave to drink gradually undergoes moral and physical degeneration.

In wartime it is inevitable that people should seek relief from strain; and there is nothing to be said against the occasional drink taken in moderation. The world would be a dull and colourless place if it were inhabited entirely by plaster saints eating dry bread and taking sips of plain water.

Health and Moral Responsibility. In wartime young men and young women are thrown into situations that encourage excess. The atmosphere of war is itself unhealthy, however much heroism it may bring out in people. Waste of lives, waste of materials, waste of money, however necessary these evils may be for the time, encourage a spirit of "Eat, drink, and be merry, for to-morrow we die". There is much less of this spirit in Great Britain to-day than in the last war. We are more aware this time that what we are fighting against is evil. Each man knows that he is fighting for the freedom of others as well as for his own.

This growing sense of personal responsibility of each man and woman is one of the good things that has come out of the war. There is one thing that can knock this sense of responsibility sideways, and that is a "drop too much" of alcohol. A doctor has no desire to moralize about this, or to preach a sermon about it. His concern is with health, and ill-health or disease. He knows, for example, that the occasional "binge" often leads to an occasional "night out" between a man and a woman who, under the temporary influence of alcohol, lose their sense of responsibility. The doctor knows, too, that casual sexual relations often end up in venereal disease. Or to put it in another way, he knows that venereal disease is almost always the result of promiscuous sexual relationships.

The Causes of Venereal Disease. Although he cannot ignore the moral aspect of the question, the doctor is chiefly concerned about the effect of venereal disease on health and happiness. He knows that it is the source of untold misery. It would not be so bad if venereal disease affected only the person who caught it. The personal loss of health and efficiency is a severe penalty, but venereal disease may affect the unborn generation. The child of a parent with venereal disease may become blind, paralysed, crippled in mind and body, a pathetic and tragic witness to the irresponsibility of its father or its mother.

Let us be clear what venereal disease is. It is an infection, just as the common cold and pneumonia are infections. An infection is an attack upon the body by germs, tiny living organisms so small that they can be seen only under the microscope. The ones that cause disease are parasites and live on the bodies of human beings and other animals. They get their food by destroying bits of what they live on. Sometimes their attack is so violent that the infected person dies.

There are two chief forms of venereal disease. One is called gonorrhoea ("the clap") and the other syphilis ("the pox"). The germs that cause these two infections are very different from each other to look at. They injure the body in different ways. But in the beginning, with very rare exceptions, these germs attack the sexual organs, and they generally pass from one person to another during sexual intercourse. The infection is kept up in a community by promiscuous sexual intercourse.

In time of war there is nearly always an increase of venereal disease. This is a serious matter because, among other things, it immobilizes man and woman power. A hospital full of cases of gonorrhoea means loss of tanks, loss of aeroplanes, loss of guns. It also means loss of happiness, loss of health, loss of efficiency.

Doctors now have better ways of treating venereal disease, especially if patients will go to them at the earliest opportunity. Clinics for the treatment of venereal disease have been set up by public health authorities, and the confidence of the patient is strictly kept. A woman who is pregnant and believes she may have venereal disease should have a blood test to safe-guard her future baby.

"Prevention is better than cure" is an old saying which is as true of venereal disease as of anything else.

It is obvious from what has been said that venereal disease can be prevented in one way—by avoiding casual sexual intercourse.

Some Sex Problems.   The sex instinct is very powerful, and in any form of society, savage or civilized, it is regulated by many customs and attitudes which make it difficult to discuss with freedom and reason.   The modern world tends to become more artificial and complicated; the more artificial our lives become the greater is the strain upon so natural an instinct as sex.   Men and women differ widely in their make-up, in the way they react, in the way they have been brought up, in the standards they adopt.   The Talmud, that collection of ancient Jewish rules of human conduct, says "Love thy wife as thyself; honour her more than thyself.   He who lives unmarried, lives without joy... All the blessings of a household come through the wife, therefore should her husband honour her".   Family life is the basis of national life.   In family life is the flowering of the sex instinct.

Anyone who is worried about sexual problems should go to his or her family doctor and talk to him frankly about them.   Open discussion is good for the soul.   Often enough difficulties and worries are greatly exaggerated in the mind of the worrier because he or she is not rightly informed about the matter in question.

7. A Word to Those Who Worry

Generally speaking, before the war there was an increase in the number of "worriers", of people who felt anxious about nothing in particular. During the war there seems to have been fewer of these people, less personal anxiety. This may be because the real danger we all face is bigger than the imaginary dangers that make people nervy. And there is a closer feeling of unity, of being together.

What Makes You Worry? It is usually the sensitive person who becomes nervy and anxious. It is not cause for shame. Such people can help themselves to some extent by seeking within themselves the cause of their anxiety. It may be envy, jealousy, or hatred of real or imaginary persons. Suspect in yourself unreasonable hatred of another person or of an institution.

Some people, as you can observe, hate any kind of authority, whether it is in the shape of a person, an institution, the Government, the "ruling class". Fortunately, for the moment Hitler, Mussolini, and

Nazism are useful (and incidentally "reasonable") targets for this kind of hatred. In his consulting room the doctor constantly sees the destructive effects on a person's mind, and indeed body, of envy, jealousy, hatred, and "all uncharitableness". He observes these, mind you, not as a moralist but as someone trying to find out what is wrong with this man, that woman.

You can take heed of this lesson and apply it to yourself. You will agree that the person who is kindly and tolerant is happier than one who is not. It is quite true that it is easier for some people to be kindly and tolerant. "It is their nature", as we say. Seeking happiness, you will strive to be kindly and tolerant. If you find this difficult, watch in yourself for the first signs of hate and envy, and nip them in the bud. Try, too, to understand the cause. If you find this difficult, talk things over, with your doctor, or at least with someone who is a sympathetic listener.

Worrying Parents Make a "Nervy" Child. Doctors believe that the seeds of "nervousness", and therefore of future ill-health, are planted in childhood. It is not so much the parent who is deliberately harsh, the obviously bad parent, who is the cause of the nervous child. Such parents are the exceptions. The "nervy" child is often made so by a parent who is over-anxious, over-conscientious; the parent who worries about every little detail, and is always expecting that something will go wrong. You know the old saying "Care killed the cat". Of course the child wants care but not too much. A child is an unstable little creature, quickly passing from laughter to tears.

What is important is to give the child a feeling of security, and this he finds in a constant atmosphere of affection and trust, tolerance and sympathy. Within this framework of security given him by the love of those around him the child needs as much freedom as is safe for him. Some parents like to encourage a child to feel dependent on them. If this goes too far the child may never quite grow out of this dependence. He will always be "tied to his mother's apron strings". So when you see your child (or your foster-child if you are one of the good samaritans who are caring for evacuees) taking a new and independent line of action that is not harmful, encourage him to go his own way, helping only when it is necessary.

Remember, an unhappy child will probably also be an unhealthy child; conversely, without health a child will not be happy.

There is one form of interference with a child's dignity that is still popular—this is corporal punishment, or, more commonly, "a good smack". A man skilled in the training of dogs has declared that a dog can be brought up by kindness and that there is no need to beat it. What good can you hope to achieve by physical punishment except obedience inspired by fear? But a long moral lecture may be even more cruel than a quick slap.

A Case for Patience and Tact. In the early days of this war, when children were being evacuated to all parts of the country, there was a big outcry because so many of them were found to wet their beds. Punishment did not do these children any good. They still went on wetting their beds. In some the cause may have been physical. In others the cause was psychological.

In very early childhood the first thing a child, or infant, has to learn is to use the chamber. The mother teaches the infant this by putting it on the pot at regular intervals, and praising it when it uses it. Some children are quicker at learning this new trick than others. But there is really nothing to boast about in this. The child that is too perfect won't necessarily be happy. So a mother should not be worried or anxious because her child does not become "housetrained" all at once. In fact, if she does get worried and shows it, the child will probably go on wetting the bed and dirtying the napkin for a much longer time. A child should not be scolded or be told that he is dirty if he makes a mess when he is supposed not to—supposed not to, that is, according to the ideas of grown-up people. The child doesn't think in the same way as you do. Why should he?

Mother and Child. The mother has a very great responsibility, and bringing up and caring for a child call for endless patience. A child's future happiness is in its parents' hands, especially the mother's. No trouble should be too great, and the young mother has to realize that she must give up many of her personal pleasures and much of her freedom to devote to her children. But this is not to mean that a mother must always be interfering with her child, must always be pursuing the child with "do's" and "don'ts". This only exhausts her and the child. Unfortunately some mothers have to go out to work to make ends meet and so have not the time to give to their children. And in wartime there always arises a demand for labour of every kind, but the Government has refrained from directing mothers into war work and has left it to them to volunteer. Don't forget to go to your doctor or the Child Welfare Clinic if you have doubts or anxieties about your child's health.

Always to be tolerant and kind to a child does not mean that you should spoil him, and let him do what he likes. There is nothing worse than a spoilt child. But parents and guardians too rarely appeal to a child's reason. More often they act as "dictators" and think that "Do it because I tell you to" is a good enough reason. It is a thoroughly bad reason. A child has a very sharp sense of justice, and if you once behave unfairly to him he will soon find out and bear you a grudge. Of course it takes more time to reason with a child. But in the long run it pays to reason patiently and to be absolutely just in all your dealings with him. It is the example you set him that will speak louder than any words.

8. Fight Disease with Hygiene

People have complained that some of the children evacuated from the slums were dirty and uncared for. The condition in which some of them had to live did not make it easy to be clean. But without cleanliness perfect health is not possible.

There were two conditions that made doctors think people weren't so clean as they should be. The first was lousiness, and the second was scabies, or "the itch". In themselves the little beasts responsible for these conditions are unpleasant and cause a lot of discomfort and irritation to the person they attack. Irritation of the skin makes the patient scratch, and so sores begin. An itching skin often means a restless night and interference with sleep.

But these pests can be more serious than this. There is a very dangerous disease called typhus, which during this war has been spreading in Europe. It has not been a serious problem in this country for something like 70 years. People catch typhus by being bitten by lice which have sucked the blood of a patient with typhus. So if a large number of people are lousy, one or two patients with typhus in their midst may start an epidemic of the disease.

Parasites Succumb to Cleanliness. A louse is an insect without wings; but nevertheless it gets about with remarkable ease. Lice live on human blood. They bite through the skin of their victims, "spit" on the wound thus made, and then suck up the blood. Some lice attack the body and others the head. The head lice lay their eggs in the hair of the victim, close to the scalp. Those eggs are called nits. They look rather like scurf, but you can't blow them off, as they stick firmly to the hair.

There is one simple remedy against lousiness and that is cleanliness. This means a bath and a thorough wash all over at least once a week. A child's head must be washed weekly, too, and thoroughly combed and brushed every night.

A large number of evacuated school-children were found to have nits in the hair. It wasn't always their fault or the fault of their parents. They often caught the lice from other children. If your child is unlucky enough to have nits in the hair, try to get rid of them, first of all by washing hair and scalp thoroughly. Then, when the hair has been dried, go through it with a fine comb specially made for the purpose. Ask your chemist for a fine tooth comb, preferably a "Sacker" or a "Binns" comb. Any old comb won't do. When you comb, remember to go through the hair close to the scalp, for it is there the lice lay their tough little eggs. If you don't succeed in getting rid of them seek advice from a Health Visitor, District Nurse, or School Nurse.

How to Avoid Infection. Scabies, or "the itch", is a skin disease caused by a tiny spider-like creature called a mite. The female burrows into the skin and, in the track made, she lays her eggs. The eggs develop into other mites. The itch mite goes for the soft skin between the fingers, on the front of the wrist, in the arm-pits, or between the buttocks. It avoids the face and the scalp.

At the moment, thousands of people all over the country have scabies. The mite passes from one person to another, chiefly as a result of close personal contact between these two people—for example, when they sleep in the same bed. So the problem is to find all those who have scabies and to treat them properly so that they shan't hand on their itch mites to others. If you, or any of your family, have the itch, please go to your doctor now. Like lousiness, it is a family disease, and it is wisest to have the whole family or household examined and treated for it at the same time. It is wise, too, to see that each member of the family has his or her own towel, hair-brush, and comb—and uses no other.

9. Stop Germs from Spreading

It is easy to see that if you have itch mites burrowing into the skin of your hand it is a fairly simple matter for the mite to move on to someone else and begin another lot of burrows. It is not so easy to see how some other infections spread.

To understand how they spread is to know of one way to prevent infections. For instance, some types of tuberculosis are caused by drinking milk which has the tuberculosis germs in it. It has been estimated that about 2,000 people, children mostly, die yearly because of drinking milk from tuberculous cows. These deaths could be prevented by pasteurising or boiling milk, or by stamping out tuberculosis in cattle. If, therefore, you can't obtain pasteurised milk (especially if you live in the country) then see that at least for the children it is all brought to the boil before it is consumed.

Tuberculosis is not the only disease spread by raw, so-called "pure milk". Diphtheria, scarlet fever, typhoid fever, sore throat, and an unpleasant disease called undulant fever may also be spread by unboiled or unpasteurised milk. As short a time ago as 1936, in Bournemouth, 718 persons caught typhoid from drinking raw infected milk; 51 of them died. After that the milk was pasteurised and the epidemic ceased. If all the milk in the country were pasteurised, doctors would have much less to worry about—and incidentally, more time to teach people how to keep well.

How the Germs Travel. Diphtheria and scarlet fever, as you may know, usually begin with a sore throat; it is more often complained of in the latter disease than in the former. These diseases are the result of infection with germs—very very much smaller things than lice and mites but just as alive. Although these infections may spread through a community by means of infected milk, this is not the usual way. The germs of diphtheria and scarlet fever attack the throat and make it inflamed. Once settled there they multiply, producing thousands upon thousands of other germs. All that is needed is a cough or a sneeze, and out these germs will go into the air, to be breathed in by some-one whose throat will probably be infected as a result.

If a child at school beginning to have diphtheria sucks his school-pen and another child also sucks it, then this is another way the germ can go on its travels. If a milk-maid with a sore throat coughs into the milk then everyone who drinks that milk (unless it is subsequently boiled or pasteurised) runs the risk of catching the sore throat—or, rather, the germs that cause it.

Germs that Attack the War Effort. It is on careless coughing and sneezing that a large number of germs rely for getting about the place—that is, going from one human being to another. This is how they travel in cases of whooping-cough, measles, chicken-pox, pneumonia, tuberculosis of the lung (consumption); and—last but not least—influenza and the common cold. Altogether influenza and cold infections cause a vast amount of illness and human suffering and unhappiness, and a vast loss of hours of work to the national war effort. The Chief Medical Officer of the Ministry of Health has calculated it as equivalent to the loss of 3,500 tanks, 1,000 bombers, and 1,000,000 rifles in one year. It may not be possible to get rid of all "droplet" infections; they are more difficult to control than the infections—such as typhoid fever and cholera—that used to come from a dirty water supply.

Don't Pass Your Cold On. One way to stop germs spreading from one person's throat to another's is to isolate the infected person. If everyone at the very first sign of a cold were to go promptly to bed and stay there for one or two days, then the common cold would not be so common as it is, and everyone would lose much less time at work. The usual thing that happens is that a girl goes to her office with a streaming cold, gives it to most people with whom she comes in contact (in bus or tube or tram, as well), and on the second day sends a message to say she is worse and cannot come. By this time, of course, she has infected a large number of people, and has made her own cold worse by going to work. And she will end up by losing more time from work than if she had gone to bed straight away.

There is an obvious way of stopping germs getting from your mouth and throat into the air around you—and that is to cover your mouth and nose with a handkerchief every time you cough or sneeze. To cough or sneeze without doing this is a rude and disgusting habit, and it is amazing how many people, through thoughtlessness, have this habit. A sneeze may, of course, take you very suddenly, and you have to cover your mouth and nose with your hand.

There is a peculiar thing about germs, and that is that dangerous germs may lodge in your throat without doing you any harm. But they may prove harmful to other people. Those who have dangerous germs about their body without being ill are called "carriers"! So, you see, it is important to cough and sneeze into your handkerchief and *not* into the air, whether you have a cold or not.

Inoculation May Save Your Child's Life. Another way of preventing infection is by inoculating or vaccinating people against certain germs. In the last war (and in the present one) our soldiers were inoculated against typhoid fever, and they consequently suffered much less from this than they did in the South African War. Many of the civilian population have been inoculated against typhoid in the past two years because the risk of contamination of the water supply is greater during wartime. Fortunately typhoid fever has not shown any increase.

Diphtheria is another disease doctors are trying to stamp out by inoculation. There are about 60,000 cases of diphtheria, mostly in children under ten, in Great Britain every year. Out of this number about 3,000 deaths occur—mostly of children under five. Inoculation against diphtheria—diphtheria immunization, as it is called—is absolutely safe and practically painless. It means little more than the prick of a needle on two occasions. Diphtheria could be stamped out if all the children in the country, or even four out of five of them, were immunized against it. It is the best present you can give your child on his or her first birthday, but every child between one and fifteen should be protected. Occasionally it does not give complete protection, but if a child incompletely protected is infected the attack is usually much milder.

Doctors have spent years and years in finding the best stuff and the best ways in which to use it. They have now got it, and that being so you should take advantage of it to save illness and lives, and also the services of the doctors and nurses, so urgently needed for war purposes. Another disease of children against which inoculation is being perfected is whooping-cough.

If you have a child or children not immunized against diphtheria, have it done now by your family doctor, or by arrangement with the Health Department at your local Council's Offices, which will do it free of charge. Don't let your children go through the winter exposed to the risk of this infection. Prevention is better than cure.

10. Help Yourself to be Well

You are saved from all sorts of infections and poisonings by an elaborate Public Health Service which you hardly ever hear of until something goes wrong. Your food and water are kept pure by a system of inspection, regulation, and control that tries—and very successfully—to prevent any harm coming to you. There are free welfare centres to help mothers, expectant mothers, and children to keep fit. Many Approved Societies will help you with the cost of glasses and with dentists' fees; if you need these things, see if your Society will help you to obtain them. But you are asked to do something yourself as well—not for somebody else's benefit but for your own. By helping yourself to keep well and free from infection you are, of course, helping other people at the same time.

What you think and how you think about your health is important. Obviously no one who is always brooding over disease can really feel well or be well, even though his organs are perfectly sound. In just the same way, a person who is ill, or has some physical disability, will feel better if he makes the most of what health he has got than one who gives in to his disability. And so, too, the man who thinks in terms of health and healthy living will feel better and fitter than the man who thinks in terms of disease.

Don't think that taking thought about yourself is morbid, "unhealthy". The human body is a marvellous piece of construction. The human mind is a most delicately adjusted mechanism. And this war has shown us once more that both are, at the same time, amazingly tough. But the young men who won the Battle of Britain did not fulfil their heroic task with minds and bodies that were untrained. To get the most out of life you must put the most into it. To live, to love, to laugh, to labour to the fullness of your capacity, get fit and keep fit.

Remember, too, that good health is not just something the young have. Each period of life has its standard of good health. The health of old age is ripeness, mellowness. The health of youth is energetic and expansive. Whatever your age, strive for the best health available to you.

Seek Health with Eagerness. The average man wants a job he is interested in, to be decently paid for it, to have a wife and family, friends, hobbies, and leisure in which to enjoy them. These, in their different mixtures, bring him happiness. Happiness, satisfaction, is what he aims at. Without good health full happiness cannot be obtained. If you want to reach happiness, to be complete, seek health with the eagerness with which so many foolish men have sought gold. Good health is the real riches: it is up to you to get it and to keep it.

The pursuit of good health can be an adventure. And in this adventure all the doctors and the health services in the country are there to help you. Don't think you are too old to begin. In this war we have all decided that this country is worth dying for if need be. It is also worth living for and working for, and to do this to the top of your bent you must be as fit as you can. And just how fit you can become you probably haven't yet found out.

Index